Urban art and design

Norman Binch

Drawing outside

These are the kinds of drawings artists do outside. They then make paintings from them in their studios. Watercolours, inks, pencils, and pastels are good materials to use outside.

Some of the drawings are done just to get information, others are used to work out ideas for paintings.

Can you tell which of these drawings were for working out ideas?

1

2

4

1. Giovanni Tiepolo (1692-1769). Houses and campanile, c.1760

2. Thomas Girtin (1775-1802). The Albion Mills, London, c.1800

3. Henry Eldridge. Old houses with a cathedral wall, c.1810

4. Paul Cézanne (1839-1906). Houses in Provence

3

Photography

Photography is an excellent way of recording information about your neighbourhood. These photographs were taken from a small stretch of a disused canal. At first it wasn't very interesting because there didn't seem to be anything there and nothing was happening. Then, by being very patient and looking carefully, the ideas began to come.

You can try something similar and see how many interesting things you can photograph.

1

3

4

2

1. Canal bridge

2. Mooring post

3. Lock gates

4. Canal side

All taken by the author

Painting in the studio

These paintings were done at a time when artists were exploring new ideas about representing what they could see. The first two are paintings of buildings as they are seen from different viewpoints and at different times.

What do you think the others might be about?

1. Georges Braque (1882-1963). Château de la Roche-Guyan, 1909

2. Robert Delaunay. Red Eiffel Tower, 1912

3. Georgia O'Keefe. Radiator Building, Night, New York, 1927

4. Paul Klee (1879-1940). Stadt der Kirchen, 1918

1

2

3

4

Other ways of working

Monet has painted the Thames at Westminster as an 'impression' of the scene at a particular time. Look at how he uses the paint to create the impression of light reflecting in the water.

John Piper is famous for his wartime paintings of bombed buildings. He uses mixed media to create the feeling of destruction and to make the broken shapes of buildings more dramatic.

1. Claude Monet. The Thames below Westminster (Detail)

2. Claude Monet (1840-1926) The Thames below Westminster, 1871

3. John Piper (1903-92). St Mary Port, Bristol

3

Interiors

Compare the two paintings of bedrooms. In what ways are they different? What do the rooms tell you about the people who lived in them?

Vuillard is not interested in the perspective of the room but in the patterns and colours of the different surfaces.

1. Vincent van Gogh (1853-90). Van Gogh's bedroom at Arles, 1889

2. Edouard Vuillard (1865-1940). Woman reading, 1896

3. Eric Ravillious (1908-42). The bedstead

4. Jan Vermeer (1632-75). Woman with a water jug

What do you think interested Jan Vermeer when he
painted the woman with a water jug?

4

Decoration on buildings

Most buildings have some decoration on them. The first picture shows how craftsmen in Nepal have decorated their window frames with intricate carvings.

The other two pictures are of a rice barn built in the Museum of Mankind in London by a group of Indonesian craftsmen. The decoration is very detailed and colourful. The cockerels standing on 'sunbursts' symbolise male aggression - cockerels fight each other.

Try to find examples of decoration on the buildings in your neighbourhood.

1. Carved window frames, Kathmandu Valley, Nepal

2. Torajan rice barn (alang), Indonesia. (Detail)

3. Torajan rice barn (alang), Indonesia

1

2

3

Pottery

There are many different ways of
making pottery. The illustration
below shows how Indian potters
turn the wheel with a stick. The
tall blue pot, decorated with
flowers was made in this way.
Do you know of other ways that
wheels are made to turn?

One of the simplest ways of
making a pot is to build it with
coils of clay.

1

2

3

This Indonesian woman is building a large pot in this way.
The pot with animals on it is decorated with white 'slip',
which is clay mixed with water so that it can be painted
on to the surface.

4

5

1. Jaipur blue vase, Rajasthan

2. and 3. Illustrations showing the use of a
stick wheel to throw pots

4. Large pot with animal decoration, Peru

5. Making coil pots, Bali Indonesia

Modern British pottery

These illustrations show pottery recently made in Britain. The first photograph shows a traditional small pottery which makes the kind of objects you might use every day. The others are examples of good quality pottery made in different ways.

Can you say how they were made?

2

3

1. Whichford Pottery, Warwickshire

2. Hans Coper. Pot

3. Jacqueline Poincelet. Ceramic Shell

4. Clive Bowen. Storage Jar, 1992

1

4

Textiles

This illustration is a design for textile decoration. You can see the repeated squares drawn in pencil and the square which shows what the colours should be.

This is a page from a pattern book used by textile manufacturers.

1. 'Omar' Design for a silk and wool tablecloth

2. Owen Jones (1809-74). Persian ornament

3. An 'Arpillera' from Peru. Appliqué

This was made by sewing pieces of coloured fabric on to a background of sacking. The method of working is called appliqué. It was made by a group of women in Peru and it is about the time when they picked prickly pears and used cochineal insects for dyeing.

Weaving

The illustration below is of a modern woven wall hanging. It is only for decoration and therefore it can be woven to create many different effects. The others are of weavers making cloth for use. What do you think they are making?

1

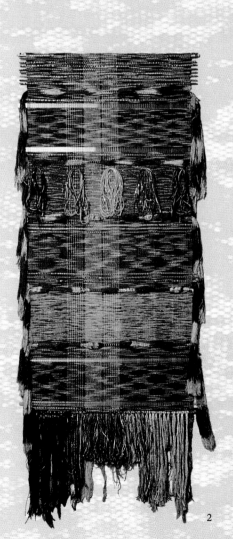

2

3

1. Weaving a narrow belt, Guatemala

2. Barbara Sawyer. Woven hanging

3. Traditional cloth weaving, Sylhet, Bangladesh

Batik

Batik is a way of decorating cloth by painting on hot wax which 'resists' the dyes. Many colours can be used and when dyeing is finished the wax is melted out of the cloth.

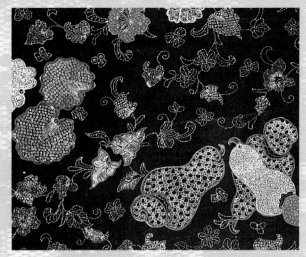

1

2

3

1. Detail of a batik sarong. Java

2. Making dyes from roots, Indonesia

3. Painting on a wax resist before dyeing, India

21

Furniture

The red plastic chair is mass-produced and is designed to be stacked when not in use. Its shape is decided by the need to stack it, but it is also a beautiful shape.

The wooden chair is hand made. Its shape is decided by the maker who is trying to create a special piece of furniture.

What are the differences between the two chairs?

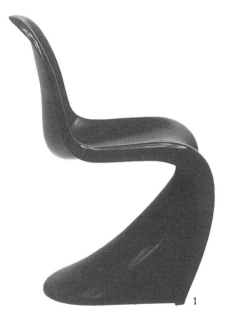

1. Stacking chair. Plastic, 1960

2. Plank back chair. Pearl Dot Workshops

Product design

These products are designed for particular needs.

The shape and size of the 'Walkman' were decided by its purpose.

The 'Robo' cassette players are designed to be fun.

Could the 'Robo' cassette players be any shape the designer wanted?

1

2

3

1. The Sony Walkman, 1978

2 and 3 Sanyo 'Robo' cassette players, 1988

New designs

These are different from the usual designs for a lemon squeezer and a toothbrush. The designer, Philippe Starck, uses his imagination to create new ideas which are very fashionable. Do you like them? If so, why?

It can be fun to think of new ideas for some of the things you use in your own home.

1

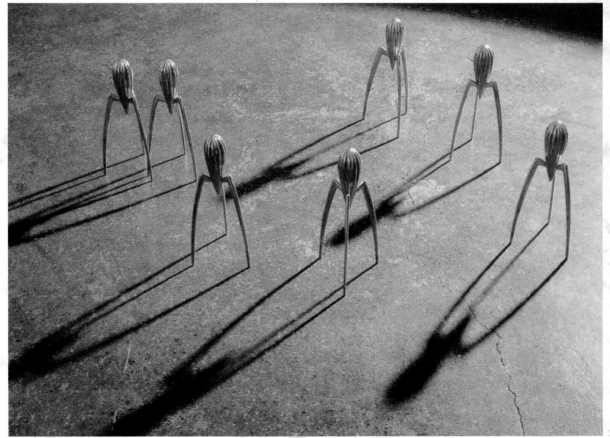

2

3

1. Lemon Squeezer, design drawing, 1988

2. Lemon Squeezers, 1988

3. Lemon Squeezer, 1990

4. Toothbrush, 1989

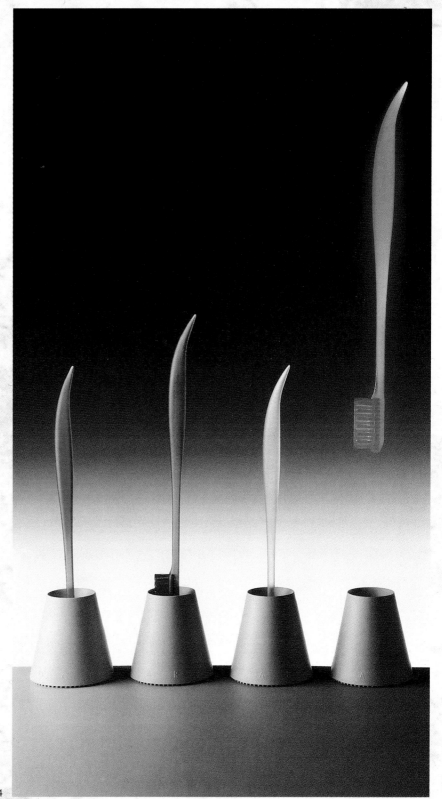

4

Graphic design

Graphic design is all around you. You can see examples in your town, on buses, on television, and on advertising hoardings.

Try making a list or a collection of as many examples as you can find in one day.

Can you say what these illustrations are? What is a logo?

1. Thomas Geismar. Mobil logo, 1964

2. Signs in Schipol Airport. Amsterdam. Total Design, 1967

3. Saul Bass. Poster for a film, 1955

4. Poster advertising an exhibition of graphic design. 1982

4

Art and architecture

Artists and architects often use the same ideas. Can you see how the abstract painting by Mondrian is similar to the chair?

1

2

Do you think that these designs for buildings and the office are also similar. Can you say why?

Try to find examples of similar buildings in your own neighbourhood.

3

1. Gerrit Rietveld. Red and Blue Chair, 1918

2. Piet Mondrian. Red, Yellow and Blue, 1943

3. Gropius. The Rosenthal Factory, 1965

4. Frank Lloyd Wright (1869-1959). Office Design

4

Things to do

Working outside

Take photographs of a small area of
your local neighbourhood. Try to find
as many interesting things to record as
possible. Use them to make a collage, a
painting or a model.

Make some paintings or drawings of
buildings using a mixture of things such
as pens, pencils, watercolours and pastels.

Try making drawings of views through
windows. When outside it is useful to
carry a little viewfinder or rectangular
frame to look through.

Interiors

Design some decoration for the windows and doorways in your home or school.

Make drawings or take photographs of details of the decoration on buildings in your neighbourhood.

Crafts and Design

Try out some of the crafts which are illustrated in this book. For example, try making some figures in clay or some simple weaving. You might need some help from your teachers or your family.

Words to remember

develop (an idea) – when you work on an idea to make it into a finished piece.

logo – a modern term used to describe a design for a letter-heading or a company symbol.

mixed media – drawing with a range of tools and materials such as pencil, pen and ink, paint, pastel etc.

perspective – making a drawing on a flat surface, such as paper, to make it look as if it is three-dimensional; – it represents what you can see from a particular viewpoint.

recording (information) – making careful drawings of things or taking photographs which record what you have seen.

representing – making an image of something which you have seen or experienced.

The publishers would like to thank the following for permission to reproduce photographs and other copyright material :

pp 2/3 *1 Museum Boyman-van Benningen, Rotterdam; 2 British Museum; 3 Private Collection; 4 Museum Boyman-van Benningen, Rotterdam;* **pp 4/5** *1 The author; 2 The author; 3 The author; 4 The author;* **pp 6/7** *1 Moderna Museet, Stockholm; 2 Solomon R Guggenheim Museum, New York/Photo: David Heald; 3 Carl von Vechten Gallery, Fisk University, Nashville; 4 Bridgeman Art Library/ Christie's, London;* **pp 8/9** *1 Bridgeman Art Library/National Gallery; 2 Bridgeman Art Library/National Gallery; 3 Bridgeman Art Library/Tate Gallery;* **pp 10/11** *1 Bridgeman Art Library//Musée d'Orsay, Paris/Giraudon; 2 Musée de Petit Palais, Paris; 3 Bridgeman Art Library/Towner Art Gallery, Eastbourne; 4 Bridgeman Art Library/Metropolitan Museum, New York;* **pp 12/13** *1 Oxfam/Peter McCulloch; 2 British Museum, Museum of Mankind; 3 British Museum, Museum of Mankind;* **pp 14/15** *1 Oxfam/Letts; 2 Oxfam/Neota/India; 3 Oxfam/Neota/India; 4 Oxfam/Letts; 5 Christine Sherringham;* **pp 16/17** *1 Photo: Rob Judges; 2 Crafts Council Collection; 3 Crafts Council Collection; 4 Crafts Council Collection/Photo: Stephen Brayne;* **pp 18/19** *1 Bridgeman Art Library/Victoria and Albert Museum; 2 Bridgeman Art Library/Private Collection; 3 Oxfam/Letts;* **p 20** *1 Oxfam/Letts; 2 Crafts Council Collection; 3 Oxfam/Caroline Lucas;* **p 21** *1 Oxfam/Letts; 2 Oxfam Photo Library; 3 Oxfam/Nancy Durrell McKenna;* **p 22** *1Herman Muller Incorporated; 2 Crafts Council Collection;* **p 23** *1 Sony; 2 Sanyo;* **pp 24/25** *1 Design Museum/Starck Presse; 2 Design Museum/Starck Presse; 3 Design Museum/Starck Presse; 4 Design Museum/Starck Presse;* **pp 26/27** *1 Mobil; 2 Total Design; 3 British Film Institute; 4 Grapus '89;* **pp 28/29** *1 Stedelijk Museum, Amsterdam; 2 Museum of Modern Art, New York; 4 Bridgeman Art Library/Victoria and Albert Museum, London*

We would also like to thank **Jeff Tearle** and the pupils of **Frideswide Middle School, Oxford,** and **Michael Mayell** and pupils of **St. Philip and St. James First School, Oxford,** for help with the Things To Do Sections. The photography in the Things To Do Sections was by **Martin Sookias and Mike Dudley.**

Oxford University Press, Walton Street, Oxford OX2 6DP
© Oxford University Press